Early ANIMAL Encyclopedias

# FARM ANIMALS

By Bonnie Hinman

Early Encyclopedias

An Imprint of Abdo Reference
abdobooks.com

abdobooks.com

Published by Abdo Reference, a division of ABDO, PO Box 398166, Minneapolis, Minnesota 55439.


Printed in the United States of America, North Mankato, Minnesota.
102022
012023

Editor: Katharine Hale
Series Designers: Candice Keimig, Joshua Olson

Library of Congress Control Number: 2022940651

Publisher's Cataloging-in-Publication Data

Names: Hinman, Bonnie, author.
Title: Farm Animals / by Bonnie Hinman
Description: Minneapolis, Minnesota: Abdo Publishing, 2023 | Series: Early animal encyclopedias | Includes online resources and index.
Identifiers: ISBN 9781098290429 (lib. bdg.) | ISBN 9781098275747 (ebook)
Subjects: LCSH: Livestock--Juvenile literature. | Livestock--Behavior--Juvenile literature. | Zoology--Juvenile literature. | Encyclopedias and dictionaries--Juvenile literature.
Classification: DDC 636--dc23

# CONTENTS

INTRODUCTION

## What Is Farming?

Farmers are people who grow plants and raise animals. The plants and animals are used for food and other products. A farmer usually lives on a piece of land in the country. This land has a house and other buildings. This place is called a farm.

Farms and farmers have been around for thousands of years. Before farming began, people moved around in search of food. Things changed about 12,000 years ago. People began living in one place. They grew plants for food. This was the beginning of farming. Farms could grow food for many people. People no longer had to travel to find food. They could stay in one place and build cities.

Farms grow the food that people eat.

## Domesticating Animals

Farmers began domesticating animals. This means they tamed wild animals over time. Domesticated animals lived with or near farmers. The animals learned that farmers would feed and protect them. These animals naturally lived together in groups. This made it easier for farmers to domesticate them.

Most farmers first raised animals for their meat and their hides. As time passed, farmers began raising animals for milk and other products. Different animals were important in different parts of the world. Farmers in the Middle East were the first to domesticate cows, goats, sheep, and pigs. In South America, farmers domesticated llamas and alpacas. Southeast Asian farmers domesticated chickens and water buffalo. Farmers in Europe and North Africa

Farmers raise many kinds of animals.

raised geese. Farmers in central Asia were some of the first to raise horses.

## Changing the World

The world has many kinds of farms. Some huge farms are run by companies. Some tiny farms are run by single families. Not only farmers raise animals. Some people raise farm animals in their backyards. Farmers play a big part in human survival today. People need the plants and animals that farmers produce. Without them, people would not be able to survive.

## Appearance

Alpacas are slender with long legs. Their small heads have large, pointed ears. Their necks are long. Alpacas are covered in soft, shaggy fleece. Their coats are usually white, black, or brown. But alpaca coats can have as many as 22 mixed colors. Alpacas are related to camels and llamas. But alpacas are smaller.

**Height:**
3 to 4.3 feet
(0.9 to 1.3 m) at the shoulders

**Weight:**
120 to 140 pounds
(55 to 65 kg)

There are two alpaca breeds. Suri alpacas, *pictured*, have long hair.

## Range

Farmers all over the world raise alpacas. But alpacas are native to South America. Most of these animals live there. Farmers raise them for their fleece and meat. Alpaca skin can be used for leather. Alpacas can live in very hot or very cold areas. Farmers first brought alpacas to the United States in 1984. In 2022, there were about 53,000 alpacas in the United States.

## Fleece

Farmers trim their alpacas' coats once a year. This is called shearing. Being sheared is like getting

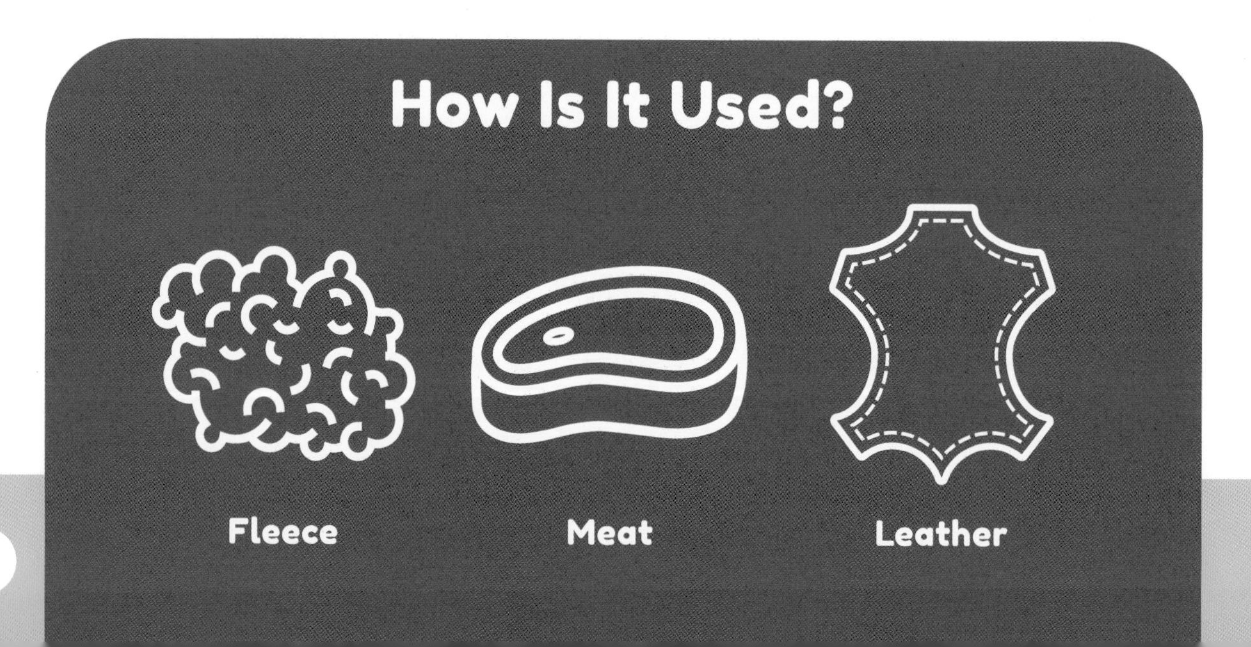

Alpaca fleece

a haircut. Each alpaca produces 5 to 10 pounds (2.3 to 4.5 kg) of fleece per year. Farmers shear alpacas in the spring. This keeps the animals cooler in the summer.

An alpaca's soft fleece can be made into yarn or cloth. The cloth is used to make clothing and other products. Cloth made from alpaca fleece is warm and lightweight. It does not irritate people's skin the way sheep's wool sometimes can. Fleece comes in many natural colors. It can also be dyed.

Huacaya alpacas are fluffier and more common than suri alpacas.

## Caring for Alpacas

Alpacas eat grasses or hay made from grasses. They also eat leaves from trees or bushes. Farmers may give them vitamins and special dry feed. Alpacas burp up some food and chew it again. This is called chewing cud. Alpacas need plenty of water.

A single alpaca is not happy to live by itself. Alpacas are herd animals. They like to be around other alpacas. Alpacas can live with llamas. But they sometimes get sick when they live with other farm animals. They can catch diseases from animals such as goats and sheep.

Alpacas are smart and easy to handle. Farmers teach their alpacas to walk on a lead. A lead is like a leash. Farmers sometimes take their alpacas to shows. The alpacas compete for prizes.

## Appearance

The bison is the largest land animal in North America. Males are larger than females. Adult bison are dark brown. They have humps on their backs. Their heads have short horns. A bison's hair is long on its head and shoulders. This woolly coat keeps the bison warm in cold winters. Bison shed their coats in the spring. This keeps them cooler during hot summers.

Bison are often called buffalo. But they are not true buffalo. Water buffalo live in Asia. Cape buffalo live in Africa. Early European settlers called bison *buffalo*. The name stuck.

**Height:**
5 to 6.5 feet
(1.5 to 2 m) at the shoulders

**Weight:**
1,800 to 2,400 pounds
(815 to 1,090 kg)

Bison once roamed across North America. Now most bison live on farms.

## Almost Gone

Bison used to roam throughout North America. In 1800, up to 60 million wild bison lived in the United States and Canada. People of the Northern Plains Native Nations hunted wild bison. They used every part of the bison for food, clothing, shelter, and tools.

Then European settlers began hunting bison for their hides. The settlers usually wasted the meat. They killed so many bison that there were only around 1,000 left in 1900.

Farmers began to raise bison to sell. Bison numbers increased slowly. By 2000, farmers all over North America raised bison. Twenty years later, about 500,000 bison were living in North America. Around 30,000 bison still live in wild herds. The rest live on farms. Most farmers sell their bison for meat. After bison are killed for meat, they can have other uses. Bison skins can be used to make leather. Sometimes bison horns are made into jewelry. Bison skulls can

People can use bison meat instead of beef in burgers.

become decorations. Sweaters can be made from bison hair.

## Caring for Bison

Bison eat grasses and hay. They also need plenty of water. Bison do not need to be kept in a barn or shed during cold weather. Their thick winter coats keep them warm.

Bison are not tame animals. If bison have plenty of water and grasses to eat, they will stay inside fences. But they can sometimes tear down fences. Farmers must be careful when working with bison. Bison are big and can run fast. They can be dangerous to farmers. A bison will fight if a herd member is in trouble.

Bison
live in
herds.

## Appearance

Two kinds of camels live on Earth. Camels with one hump are called dromedary camels. Camels with two humps are called Bactrian camels. Nearly all of the camels in the world are dromedary camels. Dromedary camels give more milk than Bactrian camels. This makes dromedaries a more popular choice for camel farmers.

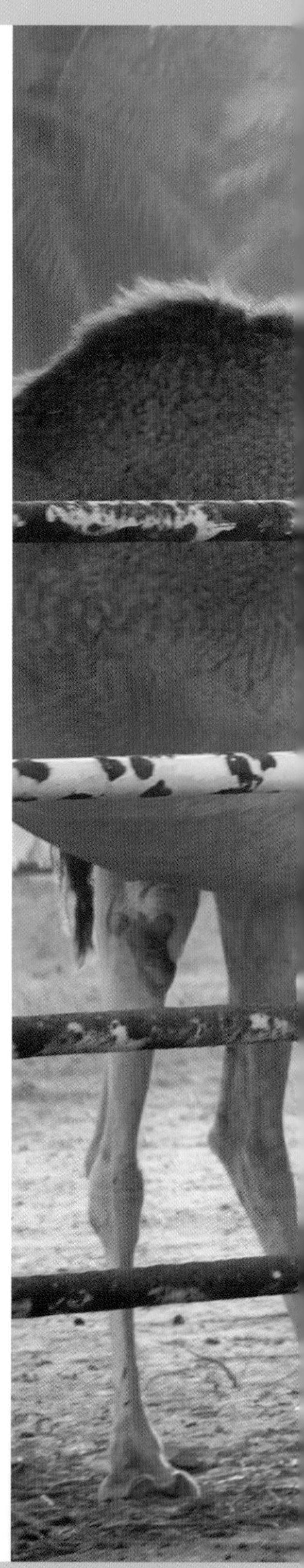

**Height:**

6 to 6.6 feet
(1.8 to 2 m) at the shoulders

**Weight:**

880 to 1,320 pounds
(400 to 600 kg)

Farmers raise camels for milk, meat, and more.

Camels are tall. Most of them are brown. But they can range from white to almost black. Camels have long, curved necks. They have two rows of eyelashes. The extra eyelashes protect their eyes from blowing sand in the desert. They can also close their nostrils. This helps them breathe during sandstorms.

## Camels on the Farm

Farmers first raised camels around 4,000 years ago. Camels provide milk and meat. Their hair can be used to make fabric. Bactrian camels are the source of most camel hair. They have longer

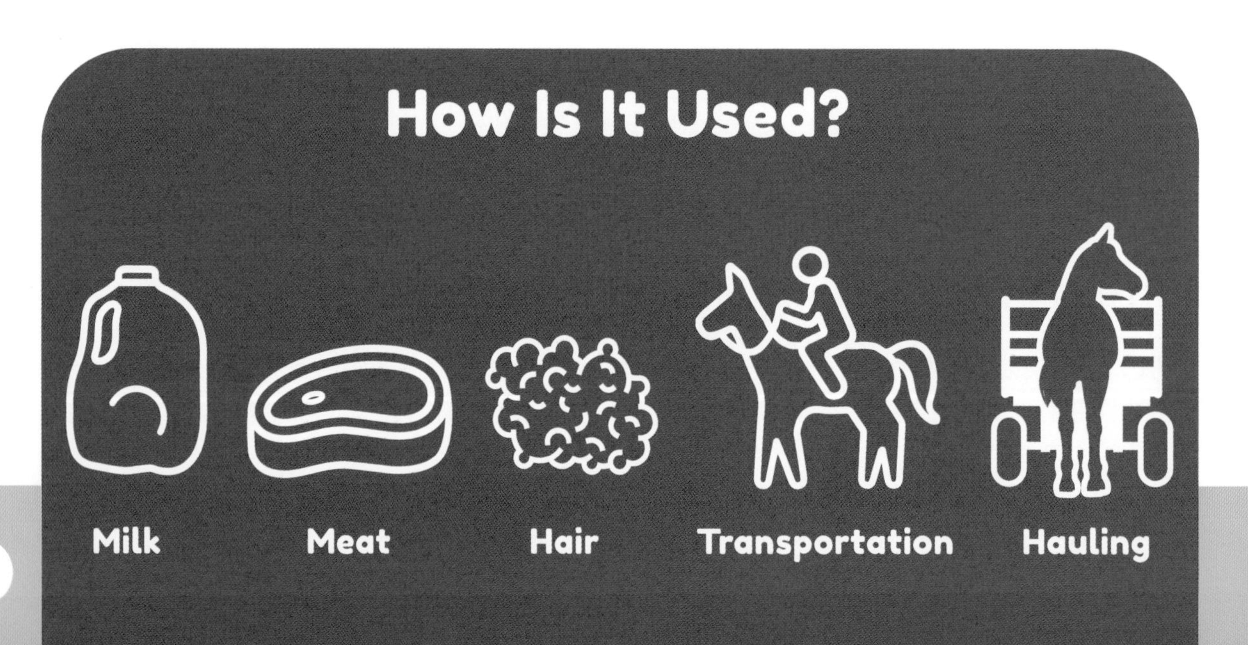

Kenya is the largest camel milk producer in the world.

hair than dromedaries. Camels are also important for transportation and hauling power. Farmers in the Middle East raise camels for these many purposes. But most camel farmers in the United States raise them for milk. Camel milk can be an option for people who are allergic to cow's milk.

## Caring for Camels

Camels will eat almost any plant. They eat thorny plants. They eat grasses and leaves.

**People can ride camels and use them to haul loads.**

Some farmers also feed camels grain, vegetables, and hay. Fruit is a favorite treat. Farmers give plenty of water and food to their camels. But camels can live for more than a week without water. Their bodies use less water when none is available. People often think that camels store water in their humps. This is not true. But camels do store fat in their humps. The fat in the humps feeds them when food is not available.

Camels need less land than many other animals. But they do not like to be in small pens. They need a big barn to keep warm and dry. Camels are smart. If they are treated well, they behave well. Farmers train young camels to wear halters. Then the camels learn to walk at the end of a rope. They learn to obey the farmer's commands. This training is important. An untrained camel could hurt people.

Bactrian camel

# Working Cats

Most cats are pets. They live in houses with people. But some cats work on farms. Many farmers keep barn cats. Barn cats usually live in barns or sheds on farms. They have an important job. They catch mice and rats. Mice and rats eat grain. They carry diseases that can make farm animals sick. Farmers want to get rid of these rodents.

Some scientists believe cats have lived with people for 12,000 years.

**Length:**
Usually 20 to 28 inches
(51 to 71 cm) from nose to rump

**Weight:**
9 to 12 pounds
(4 to 5.5 kg)

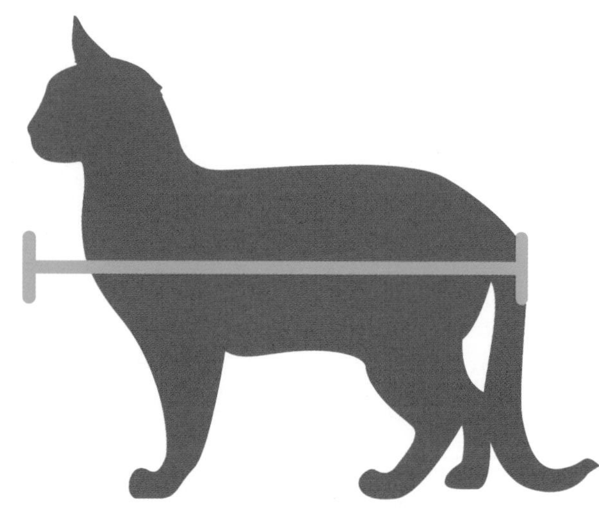

Farm cats help keep their farms free from pests.

The first known wildcats lived in Africa and Asia. Early peoples grew grain for food. Mice and rats tried to eat the grain. These wildcats came to live with people to hunt mice and rats. The cats became domesticated.

## Appearance and Behavior

Now cats live all over the world. There are more than 100 cat breeds. These breeds have many different coat colors and patterns. Their fur can be long or short.

Some cats do not like living indoors. Or they may not like to use a litter box. These cats may make good barn cats. Some barn cats like people. Others do not. But they all like to hunt mice and rats.

Some barn cats are friendly toward people. Others keep to themselves.

## Taking Care of Barn Cats

Barn cats need cat food and fresh water every day. They need a place to sleep out of the cold or rain. Their sleeping spots must be safe from predators such as foxes or coyotes. Barn cats need veterinary care. All cats need vaccinations to protect them from diseases.

Feral cats live on their own. They do not have people to take care of them. Feral cats may spread disease. They may have kittens, creating more feral cats. Controlling feral cat populations helps stop disease.

Some programs help feral cats become barn cats. Volunteers can catch feral cats and bring them to animal shelters. Animal shelters spay or neuter the cats so they cannot have more kittens. Then they help the cats find good homes. Some cats are not friendly enough to be house cats. They can become barn cats. The cats will have a warm home and plenty of food to eat.

Some farmers do not want their barn cats to have babies. Others let the cats reproduce.

## Appearance

Farmers have been raising chickens for more than 8,000 years. Chickens first came from Southeast Asia and India. Now farmers all over the world raise chickens for their eggs and meat. Some people raise chickens in their backyards.

There are about 60 breeds of chickens. Chickens can be many colors and sizes. They have rounded bodies that are covered with feathers. Most chickens are too heavy to fly. Male chickens are called roosters. Females are called hens. Roosters have much longer tails than hens.

**Height:**
Up to 2.3 feet
(0.7 m)

**Weight:**
Usually 5.7 pounds
(2.6 kg)

Pasture-raised chickens live mostly outside.

## Chickens on the Farm

Farmers feed their chickens special food. Chickens also eat insects, grains, fruits, and vegetables. Chickens do not have teeth. They swallow their food without chewing. Chickens need fresh water every day.

Some chickens are raised for meat. They are ready for market when they are six to 12 weeks old. Other chickens lay eggs. Hens lay as many as 300 eggs per year. They lay the most eggs in their first year. They lay fewer eggs each year after that.

# CHICKENS

**Some farmers raise chickens indoors to protect the chickens from predators or things outside that might make them sick.**

Most hens stop laying eggs at six or seven years old.

Some hens live in large chicken houses with thousands of other chickens. They live in cages

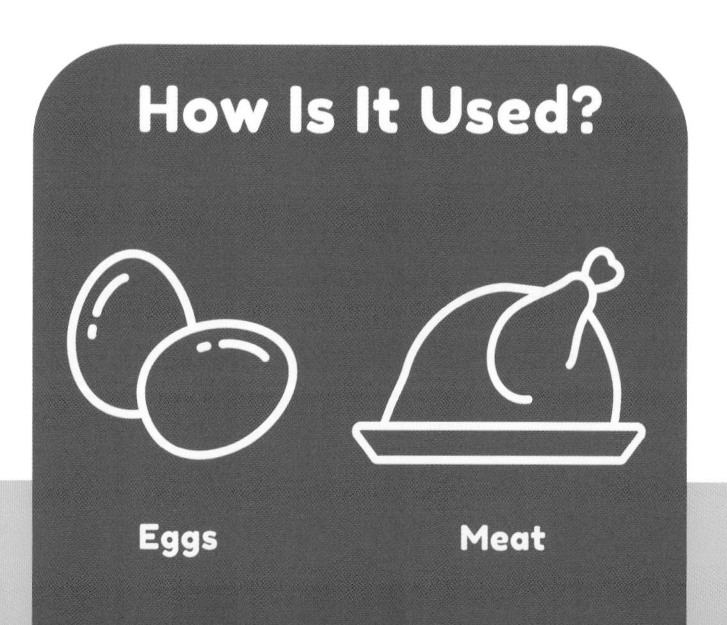

raised off the floor. This keeps the chickens away from their poop. When a hen lays an egg, it goes onto a conveyor belt. The belt takes the eggs away to be packaged.

Other chickens live in smaller buildings called coops. Coops often have a small outdoor pen. The coop protects chickens from predators such as raccoons and hawks. Hens build nests in coops. They lay their eggs there.

## Who Is the Boss?

Chickens get scared easily. They flap their wings and run if they see or hear something new. But chickens are also smart. They like people. They like to live in groups or flocks. There is usually a top chicken in the flock. This boss chicken is always first at the feeder and water. Chickens fight to decide who will be the boss chicken.

## Appearance

Farmers first raised cows 10,500 years ago in Egypt, Turkey, and other nearby countries. Today, farmers all over the world raise cows. Some breeds give milk. Some are raised for their meat. Cows can pull wagons or plows. Gelatin can be made from cows. Cow skins can be made into leather. India has the most cows. They are raised for milk there.

Farmers have many different kinds of cows. There are more than 250 breeds of cattle in the world.

**Length:**
Usually 8.2 feet
(2.5 m)

**Weight:**
790 to 3,970 pounds
(360 to 1,800 kg)

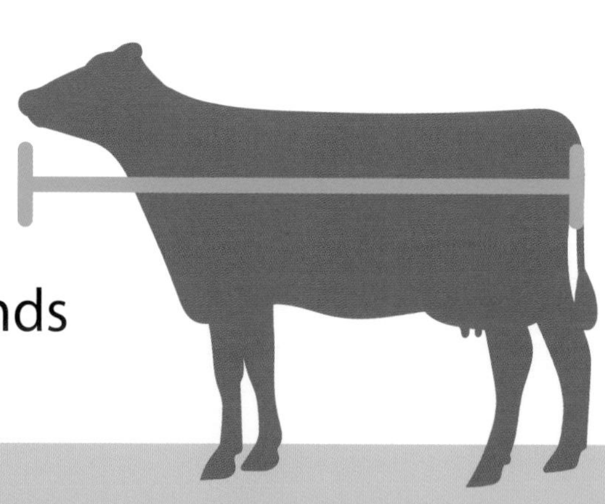

Cows
can be
many
different
colors.

Some people think of cows as being black and white. But cows can be other colors too. They can be black, red, white, or a mix of colors. Some cows have horns. A male cow is called a bull. A baby cow is called a calf.

## Dairy or Beef Cows?

Dairy cows give milk. A dairy cow will usually give 6 or 7 gallons (23 or 26 L) of milk a day. Dairy cows are females. Once a dairy cow has a calf, she produces milk for about ten months. She gives some of her milk to her calf. Farmers sell the rest of the milk.

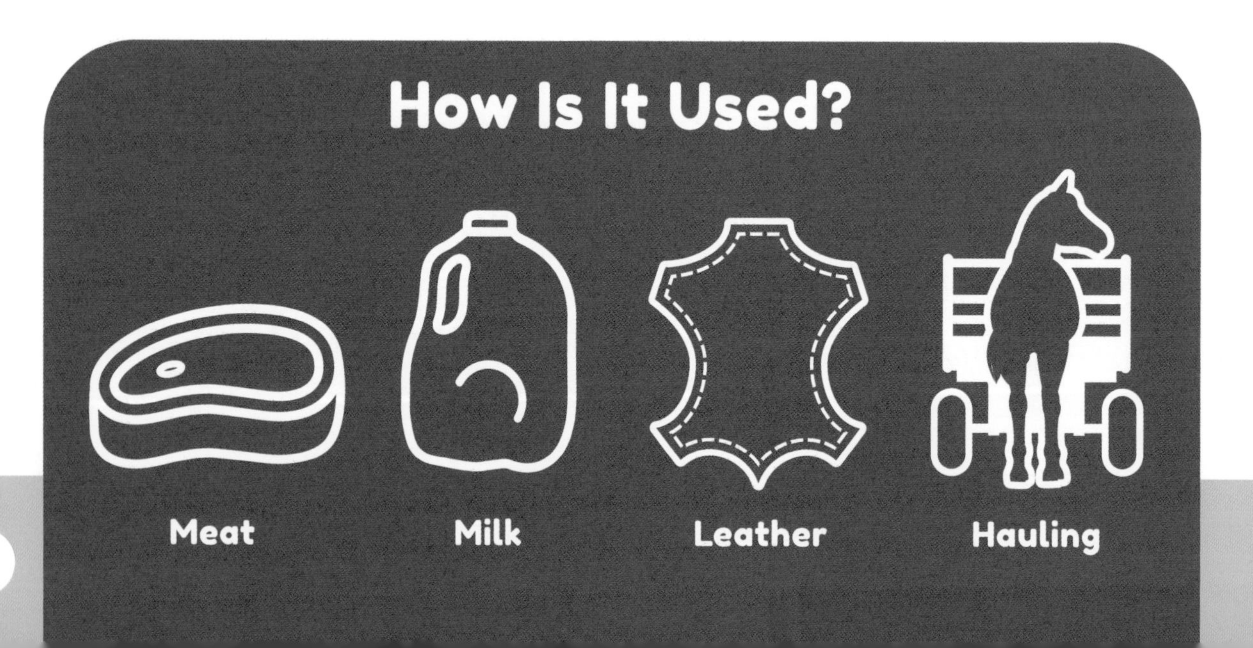

Many farmers use machines to milk cows.

Beef cows are raised for meat. Meat from young cows is called veal. People buy beef and veal at the grocery store. Beef cows are often fed extra food. They might eat grains or grasses. This food helps them grow bigger. Bigger cows give more meat.

## What Do Cows Eat?

Some cows eat only grasses. Most cows also eat hay. Some cows eat corn and other grains. Cows do not have upper front teeth. They use their tongues to grab grass. Their sharp lower teeth cut the grass. Then they chew it.

Cows have four pouches in their stomachs. Each pouch helps the cow digest its food. One pouch allows the cow to burp up grass and chew it some more. This is called chewing cud.

## Personality

Cows are herd animals. They want to be around other cows. But they often like people. They are smart and able to learn new things. They have a good memory. Cows remember if a person is kind or mean to them.

Cows
can be
friendly.

## Taming Wolves

Dogs were the first animals to live with humans. This happened thousands of years ago. Wild wolves may have first come near people to eat their scraps. The wolves learned they could get extra food by being friendly. Over time, the friendlier wolves became domesticated dogs. Both dogs and wolves are alive today. They are related. But they are not the same.

**Height:**
3.8 to 44 inches
(9.7 to 112 cm) at the shoulders

**Weight:**
3 to 250 pounds
(1.4 to 113 kg)

Farm dogs come in all shapes and sizes.

Most dogs are pets. Some are also used for hunting and other sports. There are hundreds of dog breeds. Dog breeds can look very different. Dogs can be big or small. They can be many colors. They may have short hair or long hair. Each breed may behave differently from the others.

## Working on a Farm

The breed of dog a farmer needs depends on what work needs to be done. Farmers who raise sheep or cows want herding dogs. Australian cattle dogs and border collies are good

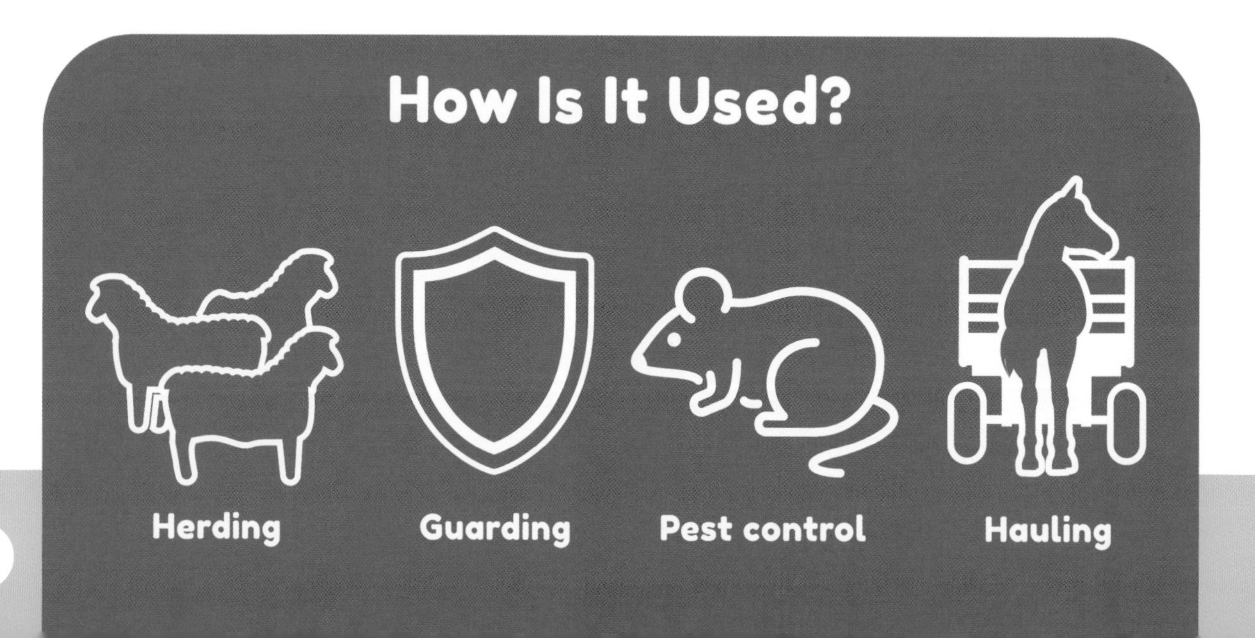

Many farmers use dogs to herd their other animals, such as sheep.

at herding. These dogs are fast.

Herding dogs are very smart. They move sheep or cattle from one place to another.

Some farmers use livestock guard dogs. These dogs protect sheep, cattle, or other animals. They often live with the animals they are protecting. They chase away predators. Large dogs such as Great Pyrenees and mastiffs make good guard dogs.

Farmers can also use small dogs. Jack Russell terriers, rat terriers, and Yorkshire terriers are sometimes called ratters. They chase and kill many pests such as rats or opossums. Ratters keep these animals from eating grains that farmers grow.

Some dogs are bred to haul loads. These include Saint Bernards and Bernese mountain dogs. Sled dogs can pull loads in areas without roads. Many sled dogs live in Alaska, Canada, or Greenland. Huskies and Alaskan malamutes are common sled dog breeds.

## Caring for Farm Dogs

Farm dogs need the same care as pet dogs. They need food and water. Farm dogs need veterinary care. They need a warm place to sleep. Most farm dogs like to be near their owners when they are not working.

Small
dogs
can help
keep farms
pest-free.

## Appearance

Farmers in Egypt and North Africa first domesticated donkeys. This was around 6,000 years ago. Donkeys provided meat and milk. These animals are strong. Farmers used them to carry heavy loads. Donkeys could climb rocky, narrow paths easily. Donkeys are still good at these tasks today.

Donkeys range in size and color. Most donkeys are gray. But they can be brown, black, or white. Donkeys have big heads and long ears.

**Height:**
3.6 to 4.6 feet
(1.1 to 1.4 m)
at the shoulders

**Weight:**
400 to 500 pounds
(180 to 225 kg)

Donkeys
can travel
in areas where
cars and other
animals
cannot.

A mule, *pictured*, is the baby of a male donkey and a female horse. A hinny is the baby of a female donkey and a male horse.

A donkey's mane stands up. Its coat can be flat or curly. It can be shaggy or smooth. Donkeys are loud. They make a noise called braying.

## Uses on Farms

Donkeys on farms help guard other animals. Most donkeys like sheep, horses, and goats. They will live with these animals. Donkeys will kick or chase predators, such as coyotes. Their loud braying is scary to predators. Donkeys also work as pack animals. This means they can carry heavy loads. In many countries, donkeys pull carts and plow small fields. Some people eat donkey meat in Italy and parts of Africa. Donkey burgers are a popular dish in northeastern China. Donkey milk is used for drinking and in skin-care products.

Donkeys eat grasses or hay. They may eat as much as 6,000 pounds (2,720 kg) of food a year. They need plenty of water. Donkeys need large fields where they can run. They need shelter from rain and the cold.

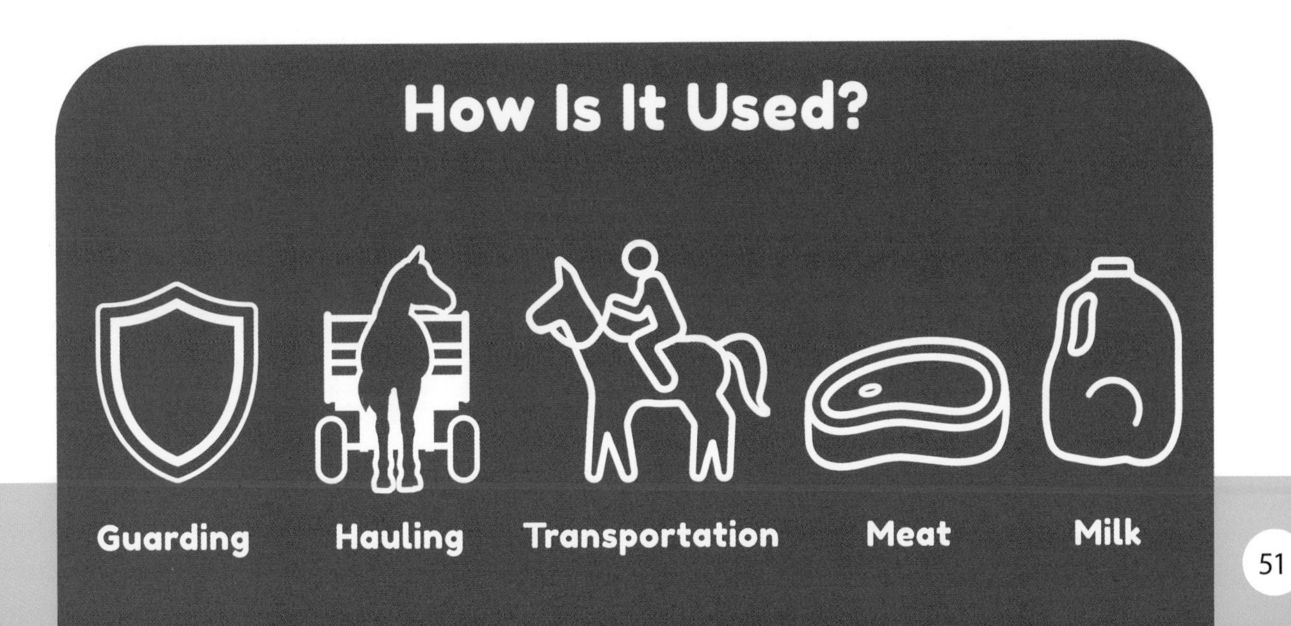

## Are Donkeys Stubborn?

Donkeys are often called stubborn. But they are really just careful. Donkeys will not obey an order unless they think it is safe. Donkeys are calm and do not get excited easily. They are patient with children. Donkeys are social. They become good friends with other donkeys. When donkey friends are kept apart, they can become sad and even sick. Donkeys are happier when they live with friends.

Donkeys are very smart. They are also friendly and playful. Farmers have found that donkeys make good friends for horses. Horses can get scared easily. A donkey friend helps the horse calm down.

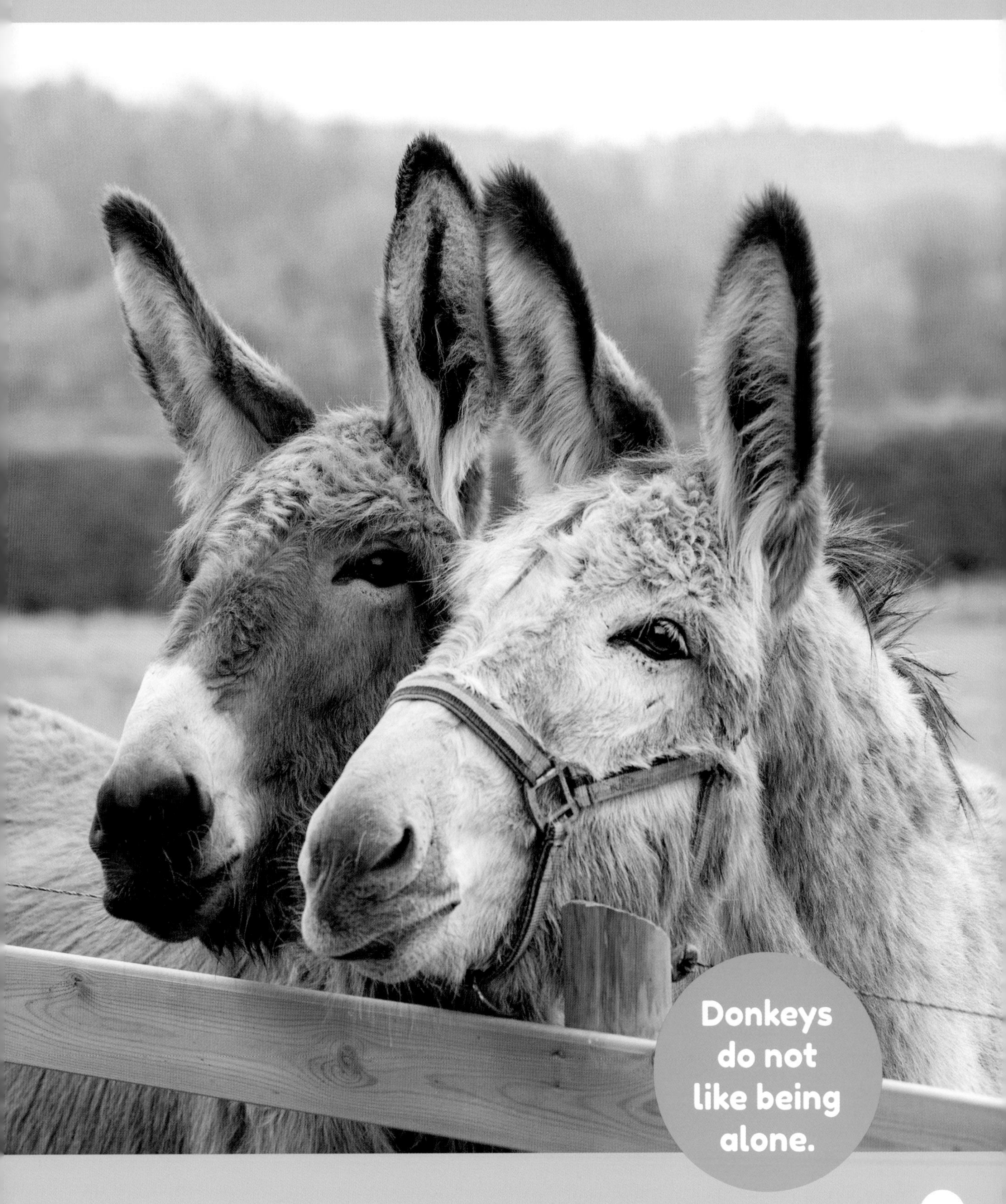

Donkeys do not like being alone.

## Appearance

Farmers raise ducks in most countries. There are at least 17 breeds of domesticated ducks. They can be different sizes. Their feathers may be brown, gray, yellow, black, white, or green. Male ducks are called drakes. A drake's feathers are more brightly colored than a female duck's feathers.

## Ducks on Farms

Farmers raise ducks for their eggs and meat. Some also sell duck feathers.

**Size:**
20 inches
(51 cm) from the top of the head to the tip of the tail

**Weight:**
8 to 12 pounds
(3.6 to 5.4 kg)

Pekin duck

There
are many
breeds of
domesticated
ducks.

Feathers can be used in bedding and for fishing lures. Sometimes farmers raise ducks as pets. Pekin ducks are the most common farm-raised ducks in the United States. Pekin ducks lay around 200 eggs a year. They are also one of the heaviest ducks. This means they have lots of meat. This makes them good ducks for farmers to raise. The Pekin duck is white with an orange bill and feet. Their babies, called ducklings, are bright yellow.

Farm-raised ducks are calm and do not make much noise. They can be raised with chickens in the same pens. Most domesticated

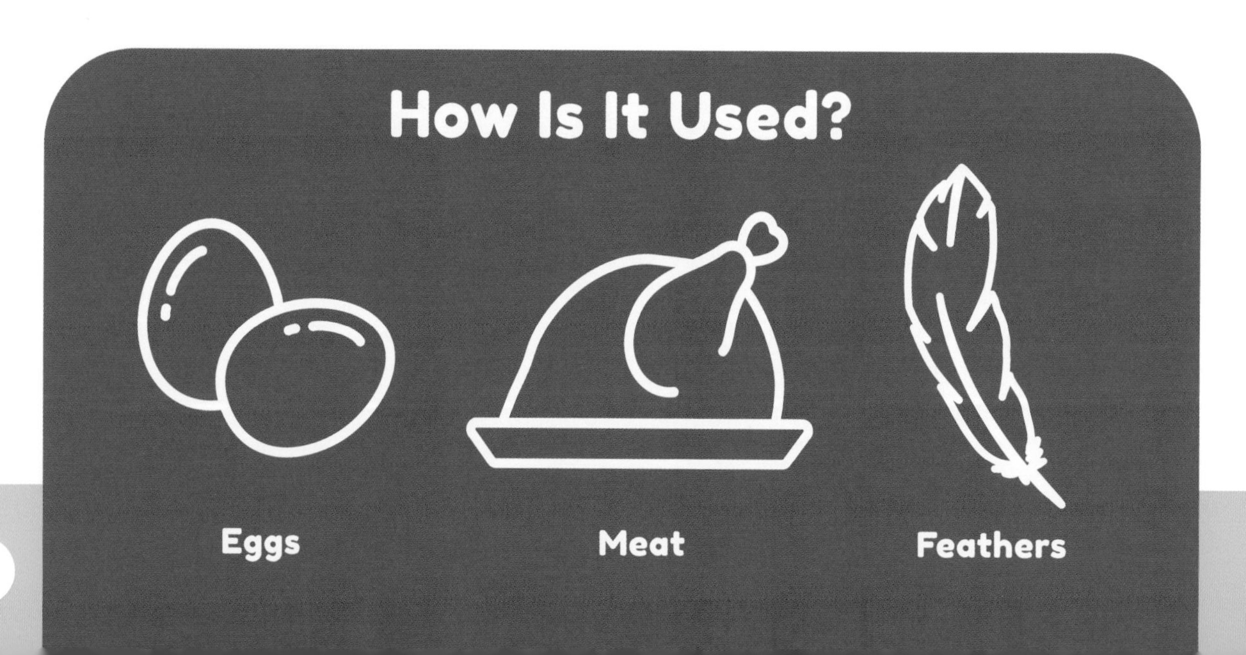

ducks cannot fly. They weigh too much. The ends of their wing feathers can also be trimmed to keep them from flying.

Duck eggs are larger and more colorful than chicken eggs.

## Caring for Ducks

Ducks eat insects, worms, and weeds. Some farmers let ducks walk around the farm. These ducks find much of their own food. Farmers give them special duck feed in the winter. Ducks need plenty of water to drink. They also like to splash around in water. Many farmers give them a plastic wading pool. Splashing in the pool helps keep their feathers clean.

Female ducks are good mothers. They protect their ducklings. They keep the ducklings close. Farmers often buy baby ducks from a farm store. These ducklings live in a small, heated area. When they are older, they move to an outside pen. Ducks of all ages need protection from predators. Many animals can kill ducklings. Weasels, coyotes, and bobcats can kill adult ducks. Farmers usually keep their ducks in a coop at night. Some farmers keep livestock guardian dogs to help protect their ducks.

Mother ducks care for their ducklings.

## Goose Breeds

Geese were first domesticated at least 3,000 years ago. Farmers raise about ten kinds of domestic geese. Most farm-raised geese are too heavy to fly long distances. But some geese are able to flap and flutter their wings for a few feet. The feathers of farm-raised geese are usually white. These geese have short legs, beaks, and necks.

**Length:**
2.5 to 2.8 feet
(0.7 to 0.8 m)

**Weight:**
8 to 12 pounds
(3.6 to 5.4 kg)

Cotton patch goose

Historians think geese might have been domesticated before chickens.

## Uses for Geese

Farmers raise geese for their meat, feathers, and eggs. Female geese lay only 20 to 40 eggs a year. A goose egg is about three times larger than a chicken egg. It is also heavier. Farmers can sell or eat the few eggs that geese lay.

Eating goose meat is not very common in the United States. But goose meat is popular in Europe and parts of Asia. In Europe, goose is traditionally served for holidays. Goose meat has more fat than chicken or turkey.

Geese are covered in feathers. The soft inner layer of feathers is called *down*. Goose down is

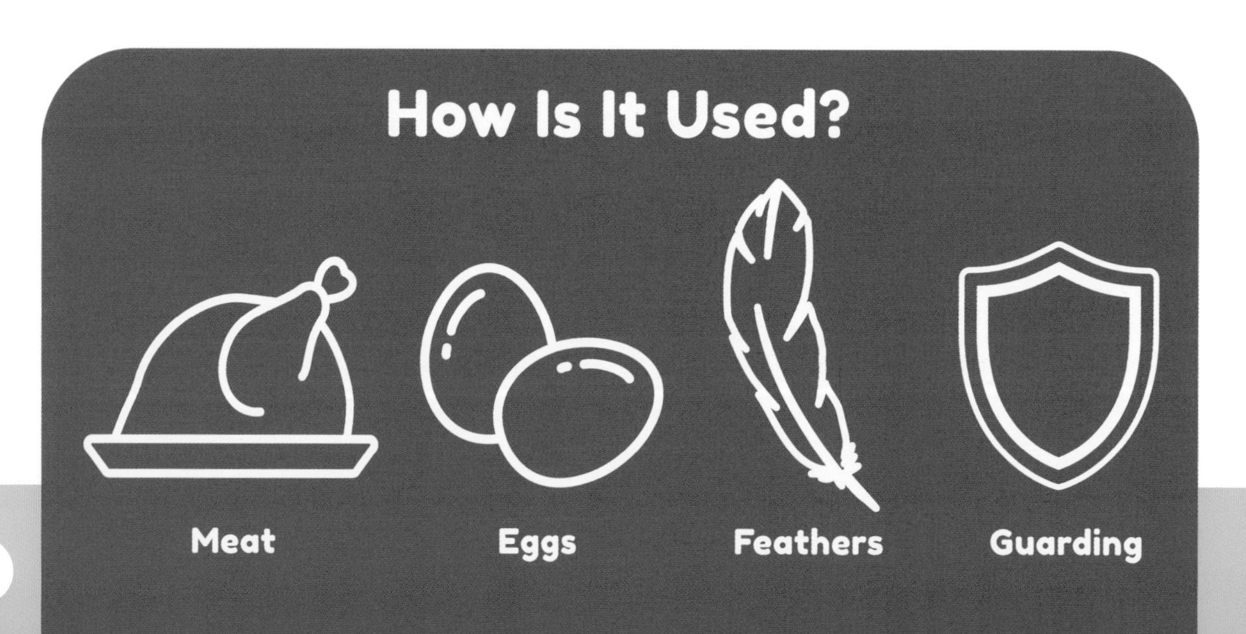

Goose down is used in bedding, coats, and more.

good at trapping heat. It is used in bedding and outdoor gear such as coats.

## Caring for Geese

Geese eat many kinds of green plants. They can live on these plants alone. But when plants are not growing, farmers may feed geese grains or poultry pellets. Geese need plenty of water. They drink and play in the water. But they also need it to help them swallow their food. Geese need shelter from weather and predators.

## GEESE

Geese are sometimes raised as guard animals. They have a loud honking call. Geese protect the other geese or animals they live with. A goose will honk loudly if it sees something out of the ordinary. It may also charge at a strange animal or person. Geese are like alarm bells. Their loud honking alerts farmers to danger.

Geese raised by farmers their whole lives sometimes think their farmer is family. Geese protect their families. They may think even a friendly stranger is dangerous to the farmer. People often say that geese are mean. But geese are only protecting their farmers when they honk and charge at strangers.

Baby
geese
are called
goslings.

## Appearance

Goats can be many colors and sizes. Their coats can be black, white, red, or brown. They can have spots, stripes, or blended colors. Their coats can be smooth or rough. Some goats have floppy ears. Others have ears that stand up. Some goats have beards. Many goats have horns. Male goats are larger than females.

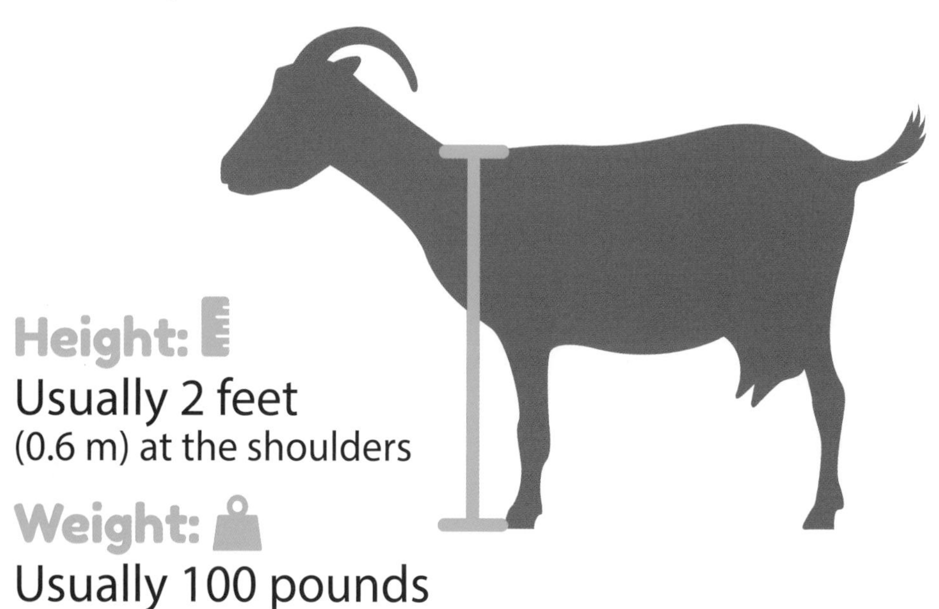

**Height:**
Usually 2 feet
(0.6 m) at the shoulders

**Weight:**
Usually 100 pounds
(45 kg)

There are many goat breeds.

## Raising Goats

Farmers have been raising goats for 10,000 years. Domestic goats are raised for milk, meat, leather, and hair. There are more than 200 breeds of domestic goats.

Farmers all over the world raise goats. Farmers need less room to raise goats than cows. Goat milk can take the place of cow's milk. The milk can be made into cheese. Goat meat is low in fat. It has lots of vitamins. People often put it in curry or stew. A goat's skin can be made into leather. This leather is soft. It can be used for gloves and other clothing. Cashmere is a soft, warm fabric.

It comes from Kashmir goats. The soft inner layer of hair from the goats is made into this fabric.

## Will Goats Eat Anything?

People often say that goats will eat anything. But this is not true. Goats are picky eaters. They may sample different foods. But they keep eating only food that they like. All goats eat grasses or hay. Goats also eat weeds, shrubs, and sometimes tree bark. They like to eat grains. But too much grain can make them fat.

Some people do yoga with goats. The goats sometimes climb on people!

## Climbing Goats

Goats want to be with other goats. They are curious and brave. They will climb on almost anything. A goat will scramble up on a shed, a tree branch, or even a cow! Goats like to be higher than anything else. Standing up high lets goats see any predators nearby.

Goats are very smart. Some try to become the boss in their herds. They do this by headbutting each other. The weaker goat will back down. Goats may also headbutt a person. Sometimes the goat does this to show the person that it is the boss. Farmers stop this behavior. A bossy goat could hurt a person. Goats are only allowed to headbutt other goats.

## Appearance

There are more than 200 breeds of horses. They live all over the world. Horses come in many colors. These include black, chestnut, bay, gray, palomino, buckskin, and dun. Horse coat patterns have special names. For example, pinto horses have patches of white and a darker color. Leopard and blanket horses both have spots.

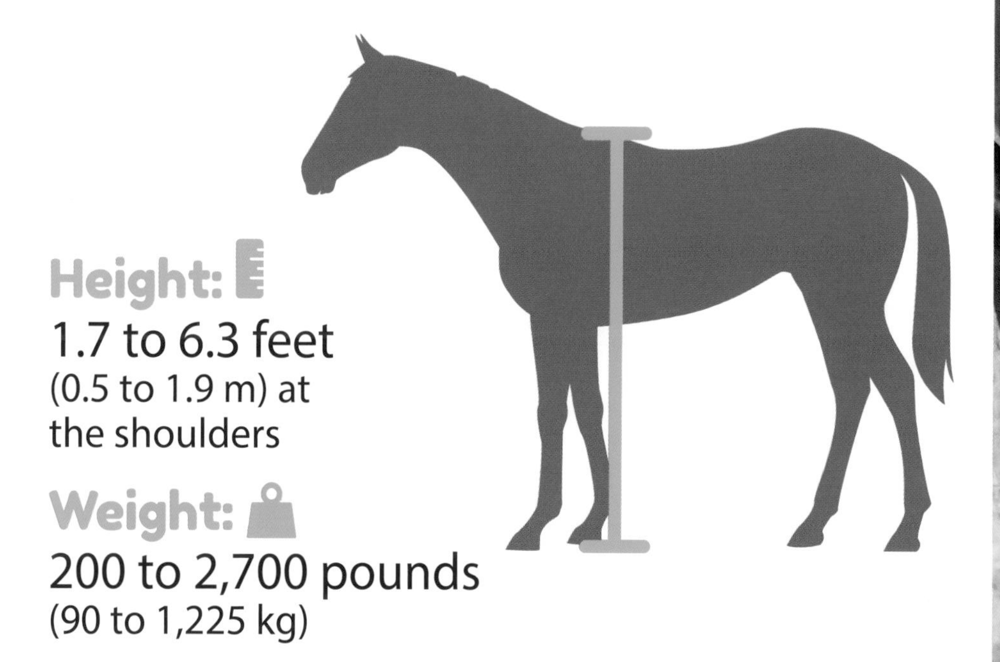

**Height:**
1.7 to 6.3 feet
(0.5 to 1.9 m) at the shoulders

**Weight:**
200 to 2,700 pounds
(90 to 1,225 kg)

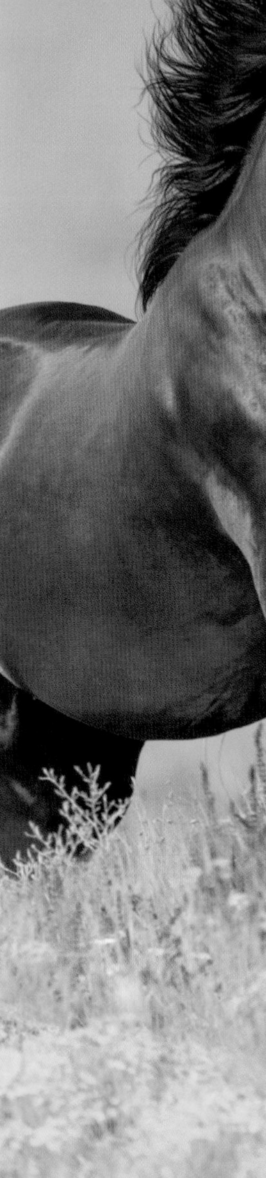

Bay horses, *left and right*, have black lower legs, manes, and tails. Chestnut horses, *center*, have golden or brown manes and tails.

Horses can range greatly in size. Horses under 4 feet (1.2 m) tall are called ponies. Ponies are not baby horses. They are horses that are bred to be small. Ponies look similar to bigger horses. They are very strong for their size. Ponies usually live longer than horses. They also tend to be smarter and more stubborn than horses.

## Horses on the Farm

People have lived with horses for at least 4,000 years. The first wild horses probably lived for thousands of years before that. Most horses today are domesticated.

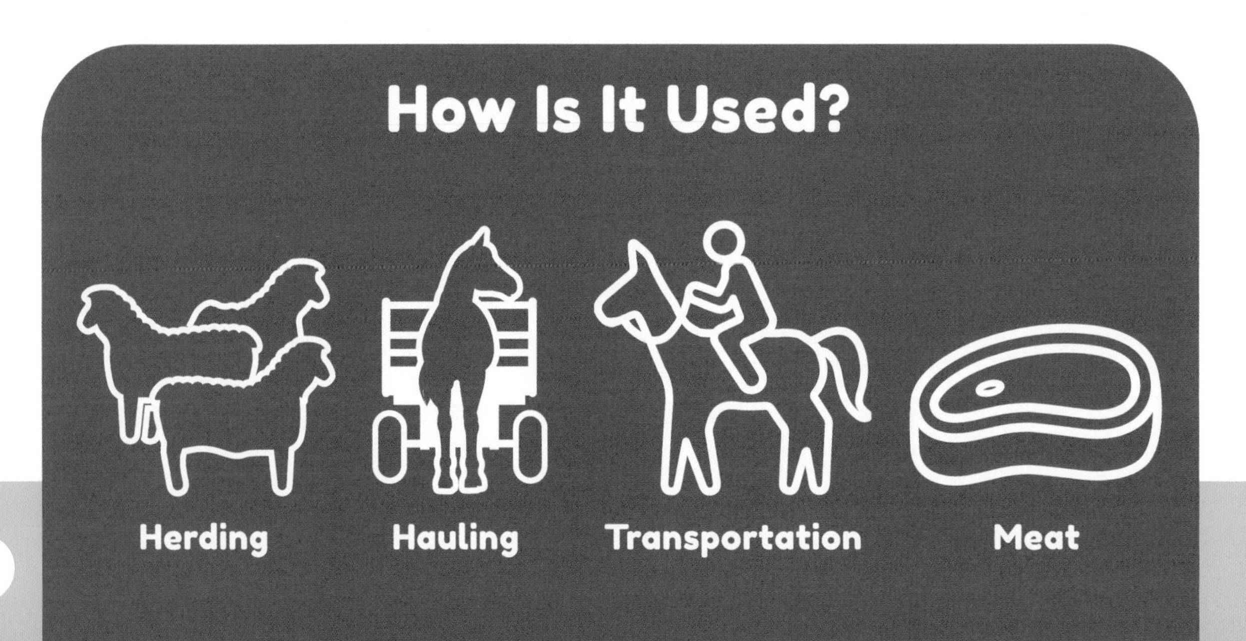

Horses can have many jobs on a farm.

Horses can be pets or working animals. Some horses are both. Farmers often keep horses just to ride. But farmers can also use horses to work. Some farmers ride horses to herd cattle or sheep. Horses can pull wagons or other heavy equipment. Some farmers raise horses for their meat. Horse meat is not common in the United States. In some countries, horse meat is illegal. But people in some Asian, European, and South American countries eat horse meat.

## Caring for Horses

Horses eat grasses and hay. They eat off and on all day long. Farmers often give them some grain. But grasses and hay are their most important foods. Eating too much grain can make a horse sick. Horses also need plenty of clean water to drink. They need sheds or barns for shelter during cold weather.

Horses want to be with other horses. A horse raised alone needs extra attention from its owner. The owner becomes the horse's herd. A horse treated kindly may become good friends with an owner. It may follow the owner around. But horses can develop bad behaviors. Some will buck or run away. Farmers correct these behaviors. A bucking or runaway horse can be dangerous to the farmer.

Farmers
can ride
horses to do
important
farmwork.

## Appearance

Farmers and llamas have worked together for about 6,500 years. Llamas first lived in South America. Now they live in many countries.

Llamas can be brown, white, black, gray, or spotted. Their coats are shaggy. Their ears are long. These animals have long necks and small heads. Adult llamas only have one upper tooth. They have narrow feet. Llamas have two toes.

**Height:**
4 feet
(1.2 m) at the shoulders

**Weight:**
285 to 340 pounds
(130 to 155 kg)

Llamas
are native to
the mountains
of South
America.

## Uses for Llamas

Llamas are very strong. They are able to walk easily on rough ground. This makes them good pack animals. Llamas can carry 130 pounds (60 kg) or more. If a llama feels its load is too heavy, it will lie down and not move.

Most farmers raise llamas for their fleece. Llama fleece can be spun into yarn. The yarn is used to make clothing, rugs, or rope. Some farmers also raise llamas for meat. Llama meat is most commonly eaten in the Andes Mountains in South America. Some people in the United Kingdom and the United States also eat it.

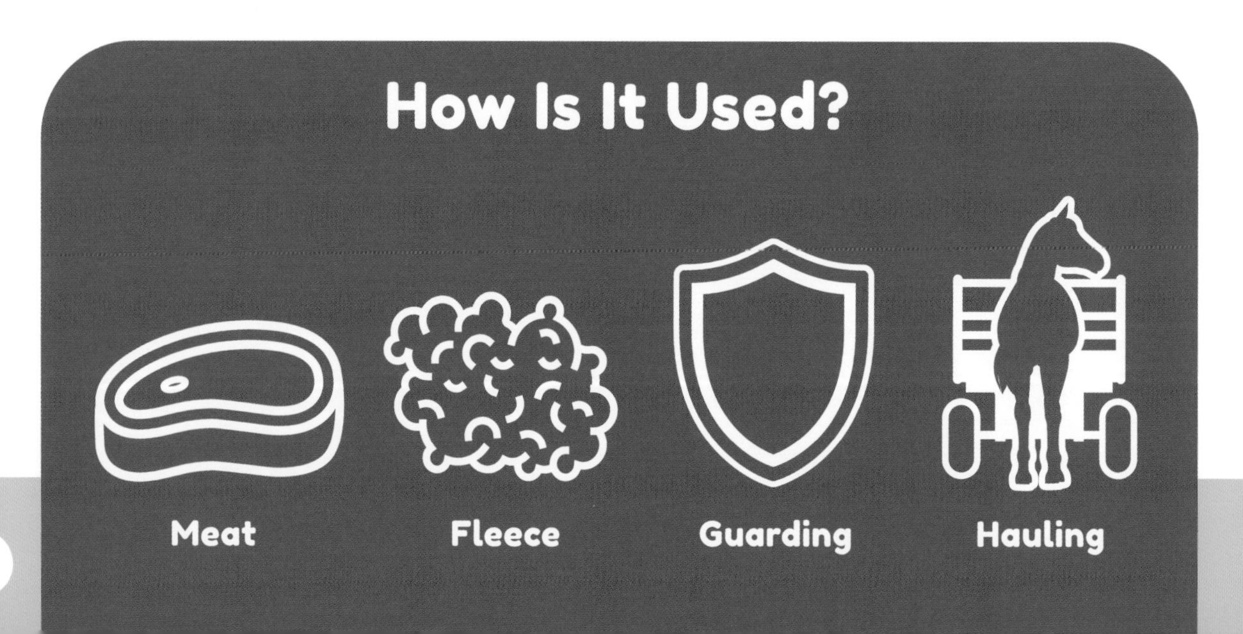

Some people in South America dress up their llamas for cultural events.

Llamas can also be pets. Some are guard animals. They protect sheep, goats, and cattle from coyotes, dogs, and other predators. Guard llamas may make loud alarm calls when they see a predator. They sometimes chase the predator. If they catch it, they may stomp on it.

## Caring for Llamas

Llamas eat grasses, hay, and shrubs. Farmers often give them vitamins. Llamas can eat 10 to 12 pounds (4.5 to 5.4 kg) of plants every day.

They do not need as much water as other animals their size. They get water from the plants they eat.

Llamas are smart and easy to train. Farmers sometimes enter them in llama shows. Llamas are gentle. They want to live with other llamas. They may get sick if left alone. They are protective of their llama families. But they may spit and push at each other to show who is in charge. Llamas like humans. But sometimes they spit at humans too. They are trying to boss the humans just like they boss their llama families.

Farmers can train their llamas.

## Appearance

Ostriches are the largest birds on Earth. Females are a little smaller than males. Males are mostly black. Females are mostly brown. Ostriches have small heads and very long necks. They do not fly.

Ostrich legs are long and do not have feathers. They are also strong. Ostriches can run up to 45 miles per hour (70 kmh). They can live where it is very hot. They need less water than most animals.

**Height:**
6.6 feet
(2 m)

**Weight:**
200 to 285 pounds
(90 to 130 kg)

Male ostriches are darker than females.

## Uses for Ostriches

Wild ostriches have lived on Earth for at least 60,000 years. People hunted them for meat, eggs, and feathers. South African farmers began domesticating ostriches in the mid-1800s. Ostrich feathers had been popular in Europe for a long time. They were used in fans, hats, and other fashion items. So, these farmers raised ostriches only for the feathers. Feathers can be taken from ostriches every six to eight months. The birds do not have to be killed. In the early 1900s, demand for ostrich feathers fell. Farmers then looked for new uses for their ostriches.

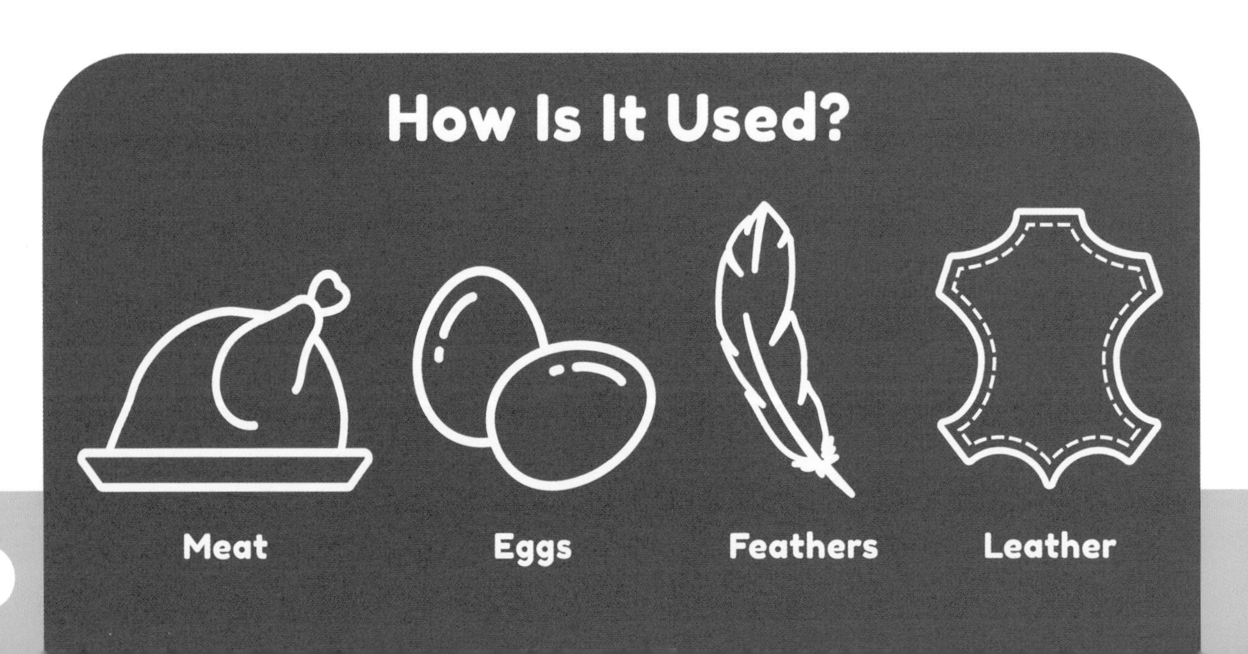

Ostrich feathers were often used to make fancy fans.

Modern farmers raise ostriches for their meat, eggs, skin, and feathers. Ostrich meat tastes similar to high-quality beef. Ostrich eggs are about 6 inches (15 cm) long and weigh around 4.5 pounds (2 kg). One ostrich egg equals 24 chicken eggs! People can buy ostrich meat and eggs from farmers or specialty stores. Ostrich skin makes thick, soft leather. It is used to make clothing and boots. Feathers are still used for feather dusters and decorations.

Ostrich eggs are very large.

## Caring for Ostriches

Ostriches eat mostly plants, such as grasses, flowers, and grains. Sometimes they eat insects. They will eat chicken feed when there are no plants. Strong, tall fences keep the birds from escaping their pastures.

Baby ostriches can sometimes mistake farmers for ostriches.

Ostriches are not usually friendly to people. They like other ostriches much more. They cannot be trained. But baby ostriches may become attached to farmers. When they grow up, these ostriches may think humans are ostriches too. These ostriches are happy to be around their farmers. But even ostriches that like their farmers may have bad moods.

## Appearance

Pigs were one of the first animals to be domesticated. Farmers raised them 11,000 years ago. Today farmers raise pigs all over the world. There are more than 300 breeds of domestic pigs. Pigs can be many sizes and colors. They can be black, white, gray, and pink. A few have some red on their coats. They may have spots or other markings. Pigs have some stiff hair, or bristles, on their skin. They have large heads and curly tails.

**Length:**
3 to 6 feet
(0.9 to 1.8 m)

**Weight:**
300 to 700 pounds
(135 to 320 kg)

Pigs
come
in many
different
colors.

Pigs do not have good ways to cool themselves off. They have to roll around in water or mud when they get hot. This is called wallowing. Pigs have a good sense of smell. They use their round snouts, or noses, to dig in the ground. They sniff out roots or other foods.

## Pigs on the Farm

Farmers raise most pigs for their meat. Bacon, ham, pork chops, and gelatin come from pigs. A pig's skin can be turned into leather. This leather is more lightweight than leather from cows. It may be used to make clothing, handbags, and other products.

Pigs are not picky eaters. Farmers usually feed their pigs grains such as corn and wheat.

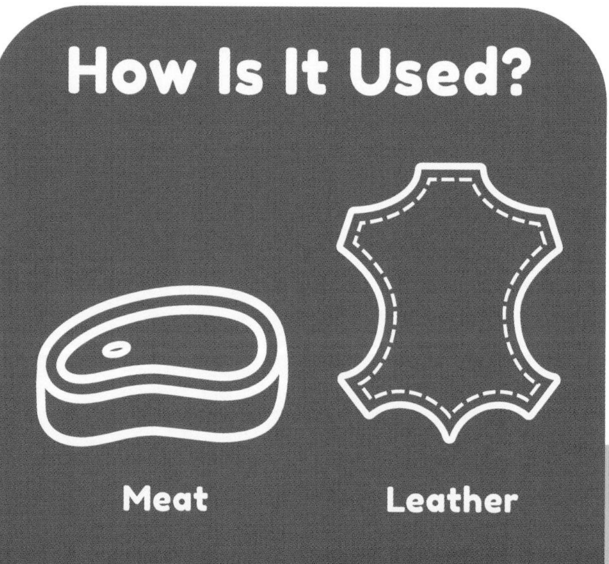

Pigs also like fruits, vegetables, and food scraps. They will eat anything humans eat. Farmers may feed them leftovers from dinner.

Pigs need shelter in both winter and summer. A simple three-sided building gives shade in the summer. In winter, they need a shed or barn that will keep them warm.

## Friendly Pigs

Pigs are very smart. Scientists say pigs may be as smart as three-year-old children. Pigs have a good memory. Pigs may grunt, squeal, bark, or scream. Each sound means something different.

Pigs are social animals. They like to play with each other. Pigs can become best friends with another pig. They like humans and can be pets. Most of the time, pigs are calm. They can misbehave when they do not have a good place to live. Mother pigs are protective of their babies. They may bark to warn farmers away or may even attack.

Mother pigs can be aggressive while pregnant and after their piglets are born.

## Appearance

Rabbits can be dozens of different colors. They can be brown, gray, grayish blue, black, white, and more. They can have mixes of these colors too. Their fur is soft. It can be long or short. Rabbit breeds can be different sizes.

## Uses for Rabbits

Farmers have raised rabbits for at least 2,000 years. People hunted wild rabbits long before that. Most farmers raise rabbits for meat. Rabbit meat is a white meat that tastes similar to chicken. After a rabbit has been killed for meat, its pelt can be saved. The pelt is the rabbit's skin

**Length:**
Usually 16 inches
(41 cm)

**Weight:**
1 to 15 pounds
(0.5 to 6.8 kg)

Angora rabbits have long, soft fur.

with fur attached. Rabbit pelts can be used for cold-weather clothing such as coats and gloves.

Live rabbits have many uses too. Some rabbit hair is shorn from living rabbits. This hair is made into yarn and fabric. Angora rabbits are known for their soft hair. Farmers mostly raise these animals in France and England. Other rabbit breeds can be used for hair too. Farmers also add rabbit manure to their gardens.

Rabbit manure is very good for the soil. Sometimes farmers sell the manure. Farmers can also sell rabbits to pet stores or laboratories.

## Caring for Rabbits

Farmers feed rabbits dry pellets. The pellets are made just for rabbits. When penned outdoors, rabbits eat grasses, flowers, seeds, roots, and tree bark. Rabbit teeth never stop growing. They need to chew to wear down their teeth. If their teeth get too long, it is hard for them to eat.

Rabbits need strong cages. A strong cage protects them from predators. They also need

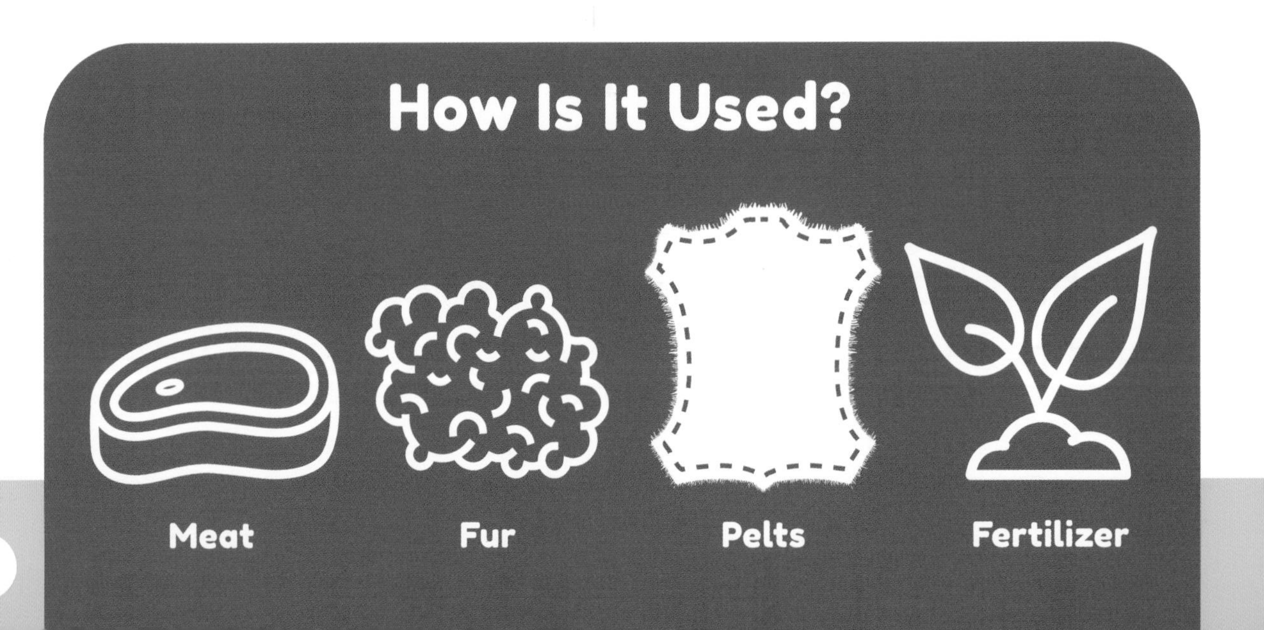

Rabbit pellets are made from hay. They contain important vitamins.

room to move around. Rabbits need shade in warm weather. Their cages have to be cleaned often. Rabbits need food and fresh water every day.

Rabbits are gentle animals. They can get scared by noises or by being held too tightly. They like humans but want to live with other rabbits. Sometimes they show how happy they are by jumping and kicking in midair. People call this happy dance a binky. Rabbits can make good pets.

## Domesticating Reindeer

People hunted reindeer for thousands of years. About 3,000 years ago, early peoples began taming wild reindeer. These people wanted milk and meat. Reindeer were also good pack animals.

Today farmers raise reindeer for their milk, meat, and pelts. Reindeer milk is creamy and thick. It can be made into cheese. But it is more often used in cosmetics.

**Height:**
3 to 4 feet
(0.9 to 1.2 m)
at the shoulders

**Weight:**
130 to 400 pounds
(60 to 180 kg)

In North America, wild reindeer are called caribou. Those that are domesticated are called reindeer.

Reindeer meat is high in protein. In Finland, people dry reindeer meat in the spring. Reindeer pelts can be made into fur boots and other clothing. The skin is used to make leather.

## Appearance

Reindeer coat colors can be dark brown to light brown to white. They have hair on their hooves. These hairy hooves help them walk on ice, mud, or snow. The hair keeps reindeer from slipping. Reindeer noses are also covered with hair. They dig in the snow with their noses to find food. This hair protects their noses from the snow.

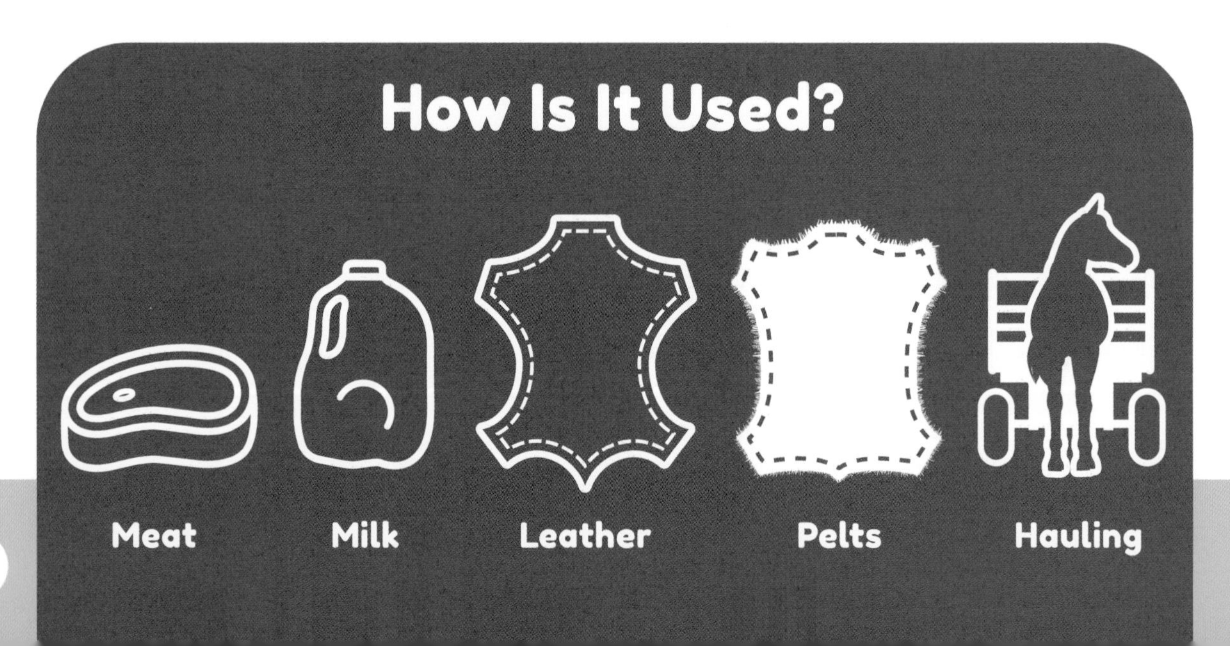

When a reindeer's antlers are growing, they are covered with soft fur called velvet. Reindeer rub the velvet off once the antlers are grown.

Reindeer have a good sense of smell. They can smell predators coming near them.

Both male and female reindeer grow antlers. A male's antlers can be 4.3 feet (1.3 m) long. A female's can reach 1.7 feet (0.5 m) long. Male reindeer lose their antlers in November. But females keep their antlers until spring. Their babies, called calves, are born in May. The female loses her antlers then. Males and females both grow new antlers in the summer.

## Caring for Reindeer

Most reindeer farms are in the northern parts of the world. Reindeer have always lived where it is cold. Their coats keep them warm no matter how cold it is. Today farmers raise reindeer as far south as Texas and Mississippi. Reindeer need shade and plenty of water in places that get hot.

Reindeer eat plants. These include willow, aspen, mushrooms, and dandelions. Fenced areas on farms allow reindeer to find these foods. Farmers also feed them reindeer pellets.

Farm-raised reindeer want to be around other reindeer. But they also like humans. They are curious and friendly. Farmers say they are easy to keep inside fences. A young reindeer can be trained to pull a wagon or sled.

Tourism and entertainment are another use for reindeer. Some people pay farmers to bring their reindeer to Christmas events for photos.

## Appearance and Behavior

Sheep have thick bodies and short tails. They have small heads. They can be different colors and sizes. Sheep coat colors range from white to dark brown to black. Sheep can have black or white skin. Some sheep have horns.

Sheep have a good sense of smell. They also have good eyesight. These senses help them notice nearby predators. But sheep have little protection against predators.

**Length:**
4 to 6 feet
(1.2 to 1.8 m)

**Weight:**
44 to 440 pounds
(20 to 200 kg)

There are more than 1,000 breeds of domestic sheep.

All they can do is move very close together when a predator is near. This makes it harder for a predator to catch a single sheep.

## Sheep on the Farm

Farmers raise sheep for their wool, meat, and milk. Some breeds of sheep can be raised for multiple products. Others are best for just one product. Meat from sheep is called lamb or mutton. Lamb comes from sheep younger than 14 months old. Mutton comes from older sheep. Sheep's milk is often used for cheese. Most milk sheep are in Europe.

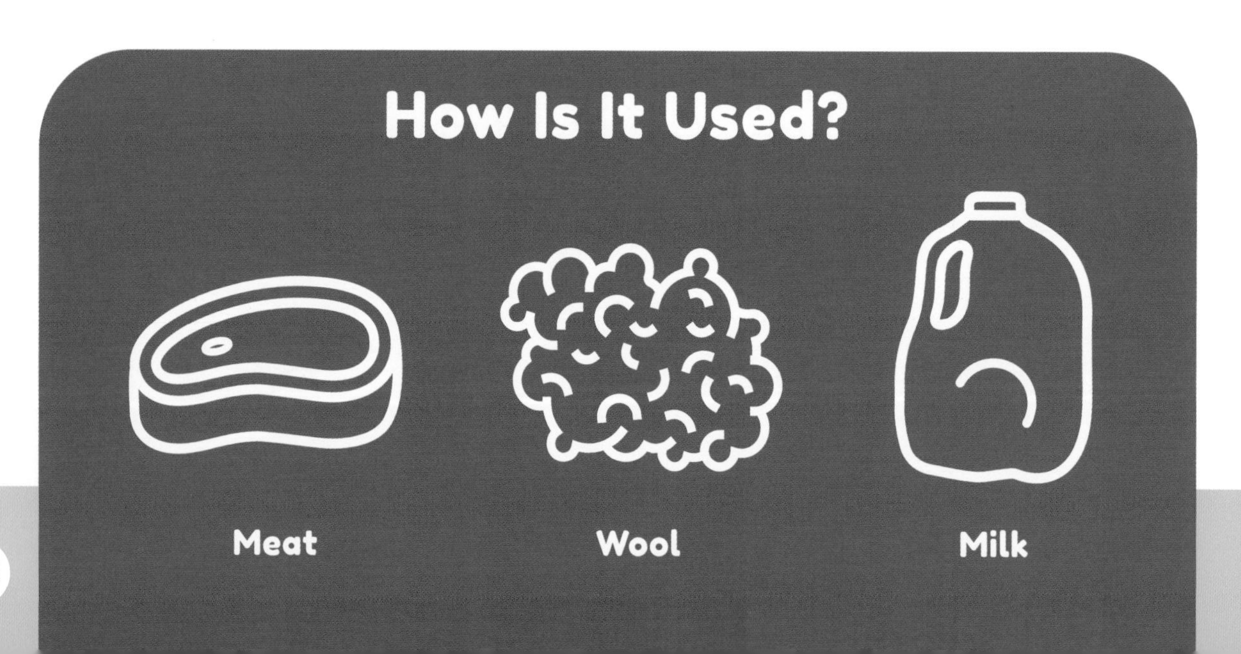

Shearing a sheep is like giving it a haircut. It is necessary for the sheep's health.

A sheep raised for wool can provide around 10 pounds (4.5 kg) of wool per year. Sheep are sheared in late winter or spring. Wool sheep need to be sheared. A sheep's wool can get so thick that the sheep cannot walk. Sometimes sheep get skin infections. Shearing a sheep keeps it healthy. But not all breeds of sheep have to be sheared. Hair sheep shed their extra hair. This makes them popular meat sheep.

# Caring for Sheep

Sheep eat grasses and hay. Sheep burp up grass or hay they have eaten and chew it again. Then they swallow it. This is called chewing cud. It helps them digest the food. Sheep need shade in the summer. In the winter, a sheep's thick fleece keeps it warm. But sheep still need shelter from winter storms. This can be a shed or another building.

Sheep move together as a group or flock. A single sheep that gets separated from the flock will cry loudly. It helps farmers that sheep need to stay in the group. If a farmer or dog gets one or two sheep to go in one direction, the rest will follow.

Male
sheep are
called rams.
Females are
called ewes.

# Raising Turkeys

Wild turkeys first lived in North and South America. Farmers domesticated them about 2,000 years ago. Wild turkeys still exist. They look different from domestic turkeys. Wild turkeys are much smaller. Their tail feathers always have black tips. Domestic turkeys have white tips on their tails.

Farmers mostly raise turkeys for their meat. Turkey is a common meal for holidays such as Thanksgiving and Christmas. US farmers produced 5.6 billion pounds (2.5 billion kg) of turkey meat in 2021.

**Height:**
4 feet
(1.2 m)

**Weight:**
17 to 30 pounds
(7.7 to 13.6 kg)

The red bit of skin that hangs over a turkey’s beak is called a snood. The bumpy red skin on its neck is called the wattle.

## Eggs and Feathers

Turkey eggs are white with brown speckles. They are larger than chicken eggs. But they have a similar taste. Grocery stores do not usually sell turkey eggs. Female turkeys lay only about 100 eggs each year. Raising turkeys for meat makes more money for farmers than eggs do. Farmers use the eggs for their own meals or for hatching new turkeys.

Some farmers sell turkey feathers. The feathers can be used in decorations. They also can be used in compost. Turkey feathers may be many colors. Some turkeys are black or brown.

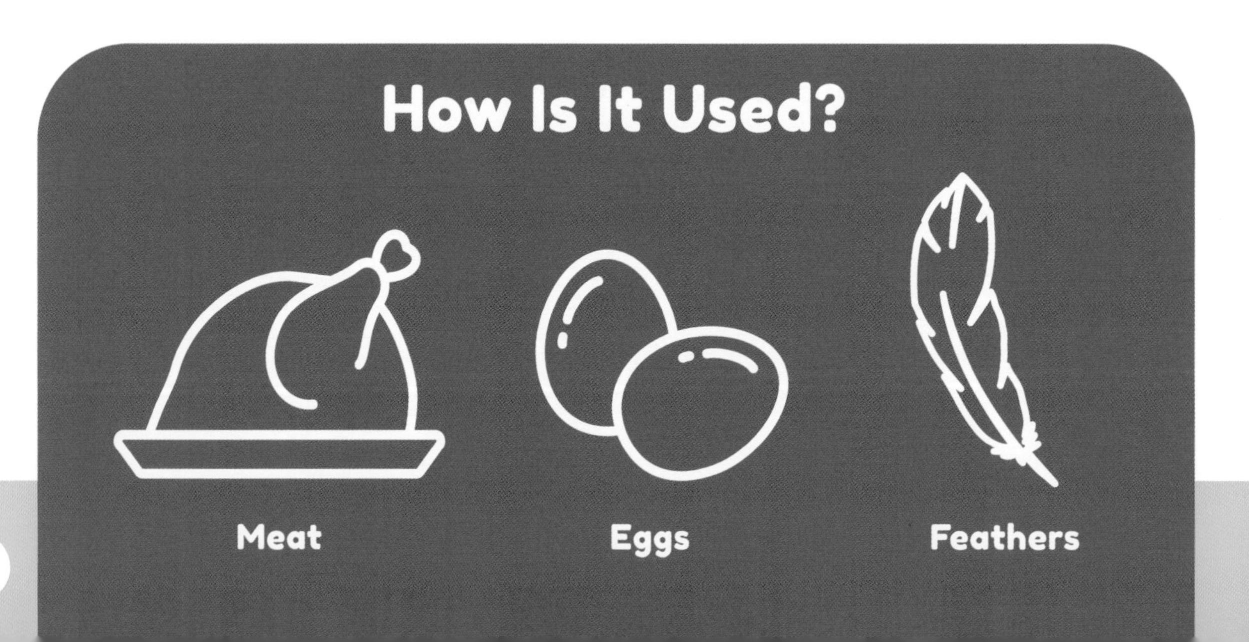

Turkeys raised for meat often have white feathers.

White feathers do not leave colors on a turkey's skin. This is why many farmers raise white turkeys for meat.

## What Do Turkeys Eat?

On some small farms, turkeys roam outside in pastures or pens. They will eat almost anything they can catch. They eat insects, berries, seeds, lizards, and more. They also eat special turkey feed pellets. Farmers make sure turkeys have lots of food. They want their turkeys to grow large. The bigger the turkey, the more money it will earn. Large farms keep their turkeys indoors in large turkey houses.

All turkeys need shelter at night. This protects them from predators such as coyotes and dogs. Their building needs to be sturdy and roomy. Farmers provide fresh food and plenty of water every day.

## Friendly Turkeys

Turkeys are smart. They are curious and like to explore. Turkeys need to live with other turkeys. They make several different sounds to talk to each other.

Turkeys are friendly, and they like people. They can make good pets. But farmers say turkeys do not make good indoor pets. They poop a lot and cannot be house-trained.

Every year, the US president pardons a turkey for Thanksgiving.

## Appearance

Male water buffalo are larger than females. Both female and male water buffalo have large horns. The horns are usually 5 feet (1.5 m) long. The horns can be curly or straight. A water buffalo's skin can be dark brown, gray, or black. The skin is mostly hairless. Water buffalo have long, skinny tails with a bushy tip.

Farmers in India first domesticated water buffalo. This happened at least 6,000 years ago.

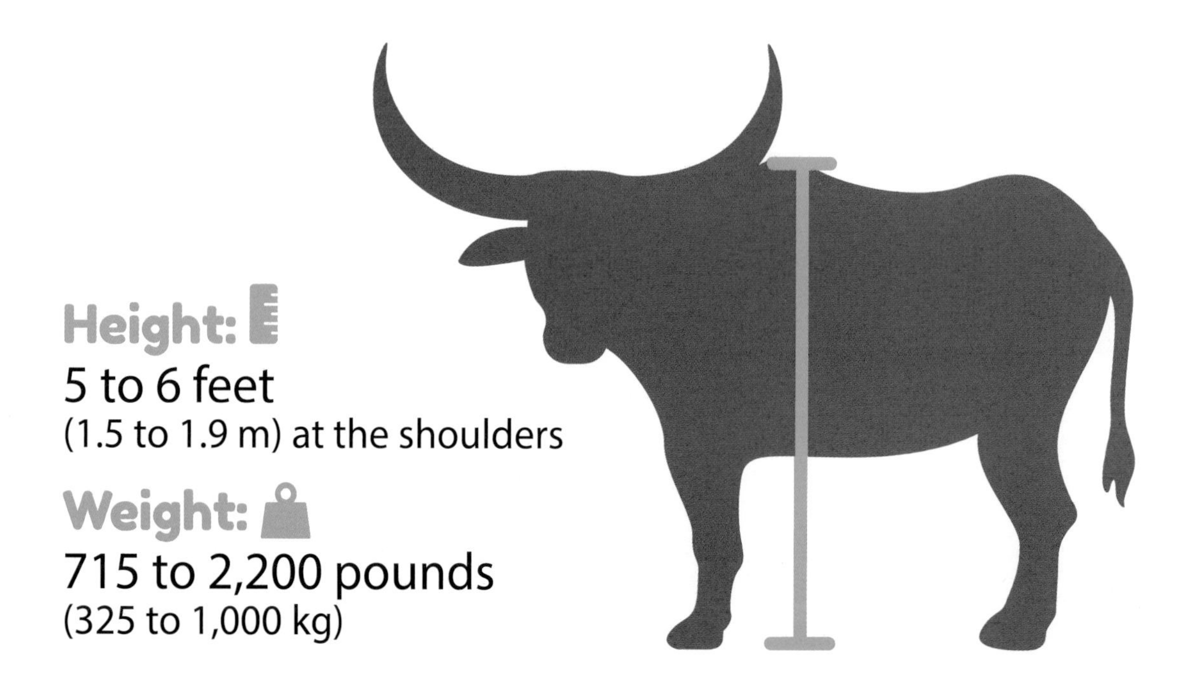

Water
buffalo
are native
to Asia.

Today farmers raise water buffalo all over the world. Most are raised in Asia. Farmers in North America, Europe, and Australia raise water buffalo too. Water buffalo are raised for milk and meat. Some farmers also use them to pull plows or wagons. Water buffalo eat grasses and other plants. They eat hay when grass is not available. They need plenty of water to drink.

## River or Swamp

There are two different kinds of water buffalo. The river buffalo is larger. It weighs about 990 to 2,200 pounds (450 to 1,000 kg). Farmers raise

Farmers can use water buffalo to pull plows.

these buffalo mainly for milk. Most river buffalo live in western Asia, Europe, and North and South America. The swamp buffalo is smaller. It weighs 715 to 990 pounds (325 to 450 kg). Swamp buffalo are mainly used to pull plows or wagons or to carry heavy loads. They are found in Southeast Asia and Australia.

Both river and swamp buffalo are raised for their meat. Water buffalo meat is tender. It tastes like beef. Water buffalo milk tastes rich and creamy. It is used to make cheeses, butter, and ice cream.

## Strong Fences

Farmers say that water buffalo are curious and smart. These animals like humans. But they want to be around other water buffalo. Fences have to be strong. Water buffalo can tear down a normal fence just to see what is on the other side.

Water buffalo often roll around in shallow water or mud. This is called wallowing. The mud protects their skin from insects. It keeps them cool. Water buffalo can live where winters are cold. But they need to be able to go into a barn or shed for shelter.

Water buffalo are named for their wallowing behavior.

## Keeping Farm Animals Healthy

Farm animals get sick. Sometimes they get hurt. Veterinarians, or vets, are doctors for animals. Most vets treat dogs, cats, and other small pets. But some are specially trained to take care of farm animals.

Veterinarians can give vaccines, help injured animals, and more.

Farmers do not bring their sick or injured farm animals into a vet's office. Instead, the vet comes to them. Farm animals need vaccinations. If they are hurt, they might need to be bandaged. If they are sick, they might need medicine. Vets can help with all of these things.

Vets who treat farm animals often have to drive many miles in a day. Some farm animals are large. Often a sick or hurt animal will be scared. It will not want the vet to touch it. A farm animal vet finds ways to keep an animal from moving too much. The vet may use ropes, lifts, or medication. Then the vet can treat the animal safely.

# GLOSSARY

**breed**
A group of animals that looks and acts similarly.

**compost**
A mixture made of materials such as food scraps, eggshells, hair, and other organic materials that helps plants grow.

**digest**
To change food in the stomach into a form that can be used by the body.

**domestic**
Living near or with people.

**feral**
An escaped domestic animal that has become wild, and its offspring.

**fleece**
The coat covering a woolly animal.

**gelatin**
A material used in foods such as Jell-O and marshmallows.

**neuter**
To remove a male animal's reproductive glands.

**pasture**
A grassy field for animals.

**predator**
An animal that hunts and eats other animals.

**shear**
To cut or clip an animal's hair.

**shelter**
A building that provides protection.

**spay**
To remove a female animal's reproductive organs.

**vaccinations**
Medicines that protect against disease, often given by a shot.

**volunteer**
A person who helps others without payment.

# TO LEARN MORE

## More Books to Read


Lukidis, Lydia. *Ducks*. AV2 by Weigl, 2021.

Salzmann, Mary Elizabeth. *Farm Babies*. Abdo, 2020.

Ventura, Marne. *Horses*. Abdo, 2023.


## Online Resources

To learn more about farm animals, please visit **abdobooklinks.com** or scan this QR code. These links are routinely monitored and updated to provide the most current information available.

# PHOTO CREDITS

Cover Photos: Dmytro Leschenko/Shutterstock, front (cow); Aksenova Natalya/ Shutterstock, front (chicken); Shutterstock, front (pig); Barbara Smits/Shutterstock, front (farm background); Eric Isselee/Shutterstock, front (alpaca), back

Interior Photos: Africa Studio/Shutterstock, 1, 58; Shutterstock, 3, 7, 8, 11, 14, 15, 20, 23, 24, 25, 26, 30–31, 32, 36, 36–37, 42, 48, 52–53, 54, 59, 60, 64–65, 66, 69 (cheese), 69 (cashmere), 72–73, 78, 81, 84, 84–85, 89, 90, 91, 93, 96, 97, 99, 100, 105, 106, 109, 112, 113, 115, 118, 125; Alena Mozhjer/Shutterstock, 4–5; Mercedes Lamborelle/ Shutterstock, 8–9; Wasim Muklashy/Shutterstock, 12; Eric Isselee/Shutterstock, 13, 18; Brent Hofacker/Shutterstock, 17; Darren Baker/Shutterstock, 18–19; Smir Omer/Shutterstock, 20–21; Ann Kosolapova/Shutterstock, 26–27; Absolut Images/ Shutterstock, 29; Wassana Panapute/Shutterstock, 33; Hendadzi Kilent/Shutterstock, 34; Ratthaphong Ekariyasap/Shutterstock, 39; E. R. Meeks/Shutterstock, 41; Jozef Culak/Shutterstock, 42–43; Dennis Albert Richardson/Shutterstock , 45; Nadia Leskovskaya/Shutterstock, 47; Ezequiel Laprida/Shutterstock, 48–49; Stephen L. Saks/Science Source, 50; Pani Garmyder/Shutterstock, 54–55; Jiang Hongyan/ Shutterstock, 57; Stefan Balaz/Shutterstock, 60–61; Zhane Luk/Shutterstock, 63; Thep Photos/Shutterstock, 66–67; Robert Michaud/iStockphoto, 70; Rita Kochmarjova/ Shutterstock, 71; Nadya Art/Shutterstock, 72; Conny Sjostrom/Shutterstock, 75; Bob Pool/Shutterstock, 77; Harald Toepfer/Shutterstock, 78–79; Hyoung Chang/The Denver Post/Getty Images, 82–83; Vladimir Korostyshevskiy/Shutterstock, 87; Valeriia Khodzhaeva/Shutterstock, 88; Helga Chirk/Shutterstock, 94–95; Blue Orange Studio/ Shutterstock, 100–101; Florida Stock/Shutterstock, 103; We Studio/Shutterstock, 106–107; Maksim Safaniuk/Shutterstock, 110–111; Chen Mengtong/China News Service/Getty Images, 117; David Havel/Shutterstock, 119; Sirisak Baokaew/ Shutterstock, 121; Pi Kei/Shutterstock, 122–123; Julia Zavalishina/Shutterstock, 124

Usage Infographics: Shutterstock, fleece, hair, decoration, pest control, herding, guarding, fur, pelts, wool, poultry meat, feathers; Malinovskaya Yulia/Shutterstock, red meat, eggs, feathers, fertilizer; Hadi Tresnantan/Shutterstock, leather; Notion Pic/ Shutterstock, jewelry; ASAG Studio/Shutterstock, transportation; Red Line Editorial, milk, hauling